HERB LIBRARY

GINGER

Kate Ferry-Swainson has been a writer and editor for fifteen years, specializing in gardening, history, mythology, and self help. As a writer she has most recently contributed extensively to *Mindpower*, a major series of self-help books; has co-written *Spirit Stones*, a book about Native American spirituality, and has written the historical section for the art historical monograph *Van Dyck*. She has also written *Herb Library: Camomile* and *Herb Library: Mint* in the same series as this volume.

Deni Bown is a freelance writer and photographer specializing in botany, gardening, herbs, and natural history. The author and photographer of *The Encyclopedia of Herbs and Their Use*, her other books include *Growing Herbs* and *Garden Herbs*. As President of The Herb Society in Britain, she lectures on various aspects of herbs and other plant topics, and has traveled throughout the world in pursuit of her subject as well as conducting specialist garden tours. She is a regular researcher and photographer at Britain's Kew and Edinburgh Botanical Gardens.

Dedication:

For Richard, Matilda and Wriggly Baby

Text and design copyright © 1999 Carlton Books Limited

First published in the United States in 2000 by Tuttle Publishing,
an imprint of Periplus Editions (HK) Ltd., with editorial offices at 153 Milk Street, Boston, Massachusetts 02109.

Library of Congress Cataloging-in-Publication Data
Bown, Deni.
　　　Ginger / Deni Bown, Kate Swainson.
　　　　　p. cm--(The herb library)
　　　Includes bibliographical references and index.
　　　ISBN 1-58290-015-9 (pb)
　　　　　1. Ginger--Therapeutic use. 2. Ginger. I. Swainson,
Kate. II. Title. III Series.

RM666.G4888 B69 2000
615'.32439--dc21　　　　　　　　　　99-042974

06 05 04 03 02 01 00　　　　10 9 8 7 6 5 4 3 2 1

Distributed by
USA
Tuttle Publishing
Distribution Center
Airport Industrial Park
364 Innovation Drive
North Clarendon, VT 05759-9436
Tel: (802) 773-8930
Tel: (800) 526-2778

Canada
Raincoast Books
8680 Cambie Street
Vancouver, British Columbia
V6P 6M9
Tel: (604) 323-7100
Fax: (604) 323-2600

Japan
Tuttle Shuppan Ltd.
RK Building, 2nd Floor
2-13-10 Shimo-Meguro, Meguro-Ku
Tokyo 153 0064
Tel: (03) 5437-0171
Fax: (03) 5437-0755

Southeast Asia
Berkeley Books Pte. Ltd.
5 Little Road #08-01
Singapore 536983
Tel: (65) 280-1330
Fax: (65) 280-6290

Printed and bound in Dubai.

HERB LIBRARY
GINGER

Kate Ferry-Swainson

Series Editor: Deni Bown

JOURNEY EDITIONS
BOSTON • TOKYO • SINGAPORE

CONTENTS

INTRODUCTION

Let me see; what am I to buy for our sheep-shearing feast? Three pound of sugar; five pound of currants; rice,—what will this sister of mine do with rice? ... I must have saffron to colour the warden pies; mace; dates—none; that's out of my note; nutmegs, seven; a race or two of ginger, but that I may beg; four pound of prunes, and as many of raisins o' the sun.

Shakespeare, The Winter's Tale, *IV: ii*

Ginger is an exotic herb whose fragrance fills a room with warmth, and whose taste warms the mouth and stomach. It has been valued as an element in traditional herbal remedies as well as a flavoring in food and drinks for thousands of years. The story of its journey to the West from India and China is an enticing saga, well worth the telling, encompassing legendary Chinese emperors, Cleopatra, Arab merchants, Marco Polo, the Crusaders, and Elizabethan sailors. And now, contemporary pharmacologists are tracing its use in traditional remedies in order to learn from ancient and tribal cultures and make new medicines harnessing the therapeutic qualities of this herb.

This book shows you how to make and use simple remedies that include ginger for a wide variety of ailments, including aches and pains, indigestion and sickness in pregnancy. It also describes how to make cosmetics and scented gifts that capture the stimulating properties and exotic aroma of ginger. Last, it gives recipes—including family recipes handed down over several generations—for traditional foodstuffs such as candied ginger and ginger beer.

ZINGIBER OFFICINALE

The genus *Zingiber* from the family *Zingiberaceae* contains about 100 species of perennials that are native to tropical Asia. Ginger, *Zingiber officinale*, is a tropical deciduous perennial, native to the coastal regions of India. It is valued for its thick. knobbly rhizome. It has erect, stout spikes of leaves growing 3–4 feet high, and in summer produces fragrant yellow-green flowers tinged with purple and yellow. Its rhizome is used in medical remedies, cosmetics, scented decorations, and for making ginger beer, among other foodstuffs. The word ginger derives from the Greek word for ginger, *zingiberis*. This in turn appears to have come from *Zindschebil*, meaning the root of *Zindschi* (India). The name of the species *Z. officinale* comes from the Latin *officina*,

Ginger growing
in the wild.

Opposite:
The knobbly
rhizomes
of coated
(unpeeled)
ginger.

meaning "workshop". It meant that the ingredient was available
without prescription, and later came to mean a plant with
pharmacological properties used as an ingredient in preparations
made by pharmacists.

Jamaica has produced some of the most highly regarded
ginger since the sixteenth century. In fact, medicinal ginger once
came from Jamaica alone; but a decline in its production and a
vast improvement in the quality of ginger being produced in
Africa led to the latter being used as well as ginger from China.
Ginger is now grown commercially in all tropical and warm
regions, including India (Cochin, Calicut, and Bengal), Africa
(Nigeria and Sierra Leone), China, Jamaica, Australia, and Florida.

Ginger is available scraped or unscraped. White ginger has
been scraped (peeled); bleached ginger has been limed; and
coated ginger has been left unpeeled. The volatile oil is distilled

from coated, dried, ground rhizomes. Ginger has between 1 and 3 per cent volatile oils, and its aroma comes from volatile oils, gingerols, and shogaols. Gingerols break down when the rhizome is dried, forming the much more pungent shogaols; this explains why dried ginger is much more pungent than fresh ginger.

Opposite: Women harvesting ginger in West Bengal.

CULTIVATING GINGER

Ginger grows in tropical climates with 1,800–2,000 mm of rainfall per annum. Pieces of rhizome, each of which has a bud on it, are planted in spring in a well-drained loam. The soil needs to be mulched to give it extra nutrients. Over the winter months or the dry season the stems wither, and this is when the rhizomes are ready to be harvested. They are placed in boiling water to clean the soil off them, and in the warm regions where they are grown they are then dried in the sun for five or six days.

In more temperate climates it is possible to grow ginger in a conservatory or heated greenhouse. It is easy to grow ginger in pots from rhizomes bought in the supermarket. Start them in a propagator or airing cupboard at a minimum temperature of 71°F. When the rhizomes are harvested, wash them, dry them in an oven that is cooling down, and put them in an warm closet. Wrap them in kitchen paper, then put them in sealed plastic bags, and store them in the fridge, where they will keep for two to three months.

USING HERBAL REMEDIES

Although ginger is safe for use, as described here, in medical remedies and cosmetic preparations, it should be used in moderation. In particular, it should be drunk in the form of tisanes no more than three times a day. Especial care should be taken with children and if you are pregnant or breastfeeding. Taken in excess, all herbs—and particularly their essential oils—

are toxic; but used sensibly following the guidelines in the following pages, ginger may be used safely.

Minor, everyday illnesses can be treated very effectively using herbal remedies. Be honest with yourself in analyzing your symptoms and the possible causes of your ailment. Herbal remedies are effective treatments for short-term complaints, but should not be used to treat ailments caused by your way of life, such as obesity, stress or depression. If you think that this applies to you, try to change your lifestyle instead. Do consult a medical, herbal or homeopathic practitioner if you have a more serious complaint, if your ailment does not improve with herbal remedies, or if you wish to seek individual advice about your particular symptoms. If you are already taking some form of medication, seek your doctor's advice before taking herbal remedies as they may interact with other medicines.

This book gives general information about how to use herbs to make herbal remedies, cosmetics, and foodstuffs. The author, editor, and publisher cannot accept responsibility for side-effects caused by taking the preparations discussed in this book.

Opposite:
Alternative medicines, including ginger, are effective and tried-and-tested natural remedies.

CHAPTER 1
HISTORY AND MYTHOLOGY

... HOT AND MOIST, AND

PROVOKING VENERIE

JOHN GERARD

Peoples of the world have been using medicines derived from plants for longer than we can ever know. Their knowledge of and skill in using plants was handed down orally from generation to generation before it was ever written down. Ginger has been used in cultures as diverse as ancient India and Victorian England, valued for its warmth and exotic flavor—and for its ability to increase male virility.

AYURVEDIC INDIA

Ayurveda is the traditional healing system of India, a holistic form of healing which treats the whole patient with nutrition, herbal remedies, massage, and aromatic oils. The word Ayurveda includes the Sanskrit words for life, *ayur*, and knowing, *veda*. This system of medicine is part of the Indian philosophy of *Samkhya*, which means "to know the truth". It stresses that the basis of life is consciousness, which leads to understanding the way the world works, including what health is and how to achieve it.

In this system of medicine, five elements are thought to comprise the human body: ether, air, fire, water, and earth. Each person has a

An eighteenth-century map of northern India showing Bengal in the north-east.

15

An eighteenth-century illustration of an *asana* practised by Hindu devotees.

different balance of these, according to which of the three body types, or *doshas*, they represent: *vata*, *pitta* or *kapha*. The aim is to keep your *dosha* balanced, in a state of *vikruti*: emotional, physical, and mental health. The elements have a hierarchy from ether down to earth, and in the Ayurvedic creation myth *vata* (ether and earth) leads the other *doshas* into the world.

The Vedic literature of India, dating from about 2,000BC, includes the *Atharva Veda*, one of the first detailed accounts of this system of healing. This literature lists over 700 aromatic plants used for medicinal and spiritual healing—including ginger. Indeed, even today within the

Two women in a contemporary Ayurvedic clinic in Poona, India.

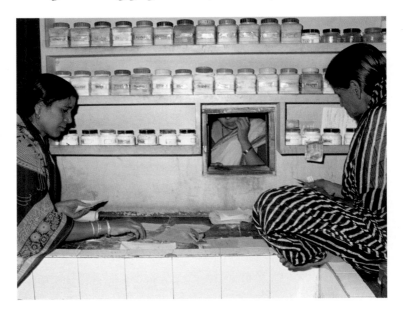

Ayurvedic system, ginger appears in about half of all prescriptions and is known as a universal medicine or *vishwabhesaj*.

The philosophy and practice of Ayurvedic medicine spread to China, Arabia, Persia, and Greece: elements of it can be found in the systems of bodily humors and elements which were developed in other cultures.

A Chinese herbal medicine text of 1739.

CHINA

Chinese medicine is considered to be the oldest documented system of herbalism in the world, with an unbroken history stretching back over 4,000 years. Chinese medicine relies on accumulated traditional practices rather than on innovation, and this accounts for its longevity.

The basic system of Chinese medicine was established 3,000 years ago (with reference to the Ayurvedic system) and is still adhered to. It holds that nature is composed of five elements: wood, fire, earth, metal, and water. The elements are responsible for our well-being and for the balance that is needed in our bodies and in nature to achieve harmony and health. Illness is caused by six evils: wind, heat, dryness, cold, dampness, and summer heat. Each element interacts with the others and is linked to one or more organs, emotions, tastes, and seasons.

One of the oldest books about Chinese medicine, *The Yellow Emperor's Classic of Internal Medicine*, was written in about 1,000BC by a number of authors in the name of Huang Di, the legendary Yellow Emperor who founded the basis of Chinese medicine. He was supposed to have lived from about 2,697 to 259BC. This is the first documentation of the principles of health and describes herbal remedies, including those using ginger.

The legendary Yellow Emperor Huang Di, and Shen Nong, the god of medicine.

During the Han dynasty of AD25–220, the *Shen Nong Canon of Herbs* was written by a number of people and attributed to the legendary emperor Shen Nong who was believed to have lived about 3,000BC. The Yellow Emperor and Shen Nong were Taoists. They advocated that people should embrace virtue in order to live long and to prosper, and believed that herbs would help them in their striving to live virtuously.

The theory of yin and yang is important in Chinese medicine, opposites needing to be in harmony to achieve health and well-being. Ill-health comes about by excessive yang (activity) or yin (congestion). According to Nei Jing, writing in the first century BC, the Yellow Emperor said "Yin/Yang are the way of Heaven and Earth, the great principle and outline of everything, the parents of change, the root and source of life and death, the palace of gods. Treatment of disease should be based upon [their] roots."

Harmony as represented by the yin/yang symbol.

Herbs are classified according to how they are considered to act upon the body: the yin/yang; *Qi* (the energy that is inherent in everything); *Xue* (blood); or the organs. They are also classified in terms of whether they are bitter, sweet, acrid, salty, or sour to the taste. Herbs are considered more potent in mixtures than on their own, as the interaction between the ingredients is thought to strengthen the whole.

Chinese traditional medicine had an important influence on the development of herbal medicine in the West. Beliefs about the origins of disease, as well as knowledge of plants and recipes for treatment, were carried westwards along the silk and spice routes.

By the eighth century AD the Chinese national custom of tea drinking was firmly established. Tea often had ginger and tangerine peel added to it for extra taste and aroma.

In the early twentieth century, traditional medicine started to fall out of favor in China, as modern medicine began to be seen as the superior system. (In much the same way, traditional herbalism became less popular in the West.) However, the 1960s saw a revival in interest in traditional Chinese medicine, and *The Atlas of Commonly Used Chinese Traditional Drugs* was compiled and published by the Chinese Academy of Sciences in 1970. Now ginger occurs in about 50 per cent of all prescriptions in Chinese medicine.

Above:
Li Bai
drinking tea.

Right:
An illustration
from *The Art of
Perfume* (1912)
showing people
being anointed
with a perfumed
herbal mixture in
ancient Rome.

THE GREEKS AND ROMANS

Fragrant herbs and spices reached the ancient Greeks and Romans from the Orient. They used aromatics on a large scale—and paid handsomely for them. At this time no distinction was made between using herbs as medicine and as a cosmetic: both were considered equally important. Wealthy Greeks and Romans liked to take aromatic baths and

fragrant massages, and Roman baths—in which aromatic oils could be applied and enjoyed—were built all over the Empire.

Mithradates orders a mercenary to kill him with a sword after poison has killed his companions but not himself.

Exotic mixtures including herbs such as ginger were reputed to have miraculous effects. The Roman Mithradates VI Eupator, King of Pontus, suspected that he was being poisoned by ambitious relatives when his food started to take on a strange taste. He took a potion called the Mithradatium specially made for him, which contained 36 ingredients including ginger, cinnamon, frankincense, and myrrh. He induced his tolerance to poisons by gradually increasing the dose (and was the first person to discover that tolerance could be acquired in this way). However, when he was subsequently deposed he wanted to kill himself by poison but found that none would work. Instead, he had to resort to the sword. In another part of

The Banquet of Antony and Cleopatra by Francesco Trevisani, showing Cleopatra proferring a drink to Antony.

the known Roman world, Cleopatra reputedly wooed Mark Antony with a potion that included nutmeg, ginger, and mace. Did she wish to lure him with the exotic aroma, or did she wish to enhance his virility?

Gaius Plinius Secundus, philosopher and author of Historia naturalis.

By AD110, Chinese ginger was regularly being transported from Luoyang by caravan along with cinnamon and silk to Central Asia, where it was traded for precious goods from Rome including gold and silver, coral and intaglio gems. And by AD200, the Romans had to pay a tax on ginger. Gaius Plinius Secundus—Pliny the Elder—was a philosopher whose *Historia naturalis* is a compilation of all the knowledge of the time, rather in the form of an encyclopedia. It mentions all the plants to which he found reference in any book of the time. He noted in AD77 that the Romans had a passion for ginger and admired its fragrance for its overtones of Oriental mystery.

THE ARAB WORLD

By AD1,000, Arabia led the world in the trade in perfumes. Raw materials were transported from India and China, to Egypt and Syria to be traded throughout the known world. Arab merchants

Venetians trading with Arabs in the Levant.

played an invaluable role in bringing back exotic herbs and spices from China to the West, and by the ninth century they controlled the spice routes and commanded prices as high as they dared for commodities such as ginger. In the eleventh century, the Chinese began trading with foreigners, and the Muslim merchants flocked to do business.

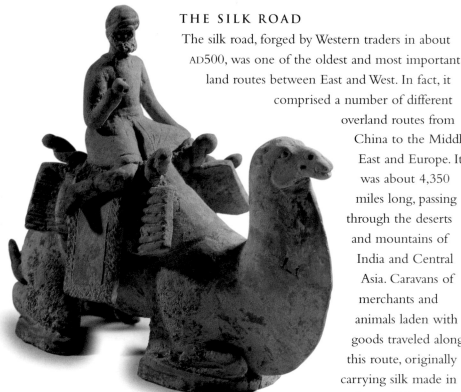

THE SILK ROAD

The silk road, forged by Western traders in about AD500, was one of the oldest and most important land routes between East and West. In fact, it comprised a number of different overland routes from China to the Middle East and Europe. It was about 4,350 miles long, passing through the deserts and mountains of India and Central Asia. Caravans of merchants and animals laden with goods traveled along this route, originally carrying silk made in northern China. The journey was normally made in relays by merchants who would travel their own known stretch of the road in order to avoid dangers—including hostile rulers demanding exorbitant tolls. Spices and herbs from the Orient were a highly cost-effective commodity to transport West: high in value, lightweight, easy to divide into loads, and with a captive market in the West.

A terracotta funerary statue of a camel and driver from Central Asia of the sixth century AD.

Right: Ruins of the ancient Taug city of Gaochang, an outlying staging post on the silk road.

The silk road was used until about 1650 when new sea routes came into use.

MARCO POLO

The Venetian explorer Marco Polo (1254–1324) was the first person to travel the entire length of the silk road, a journey

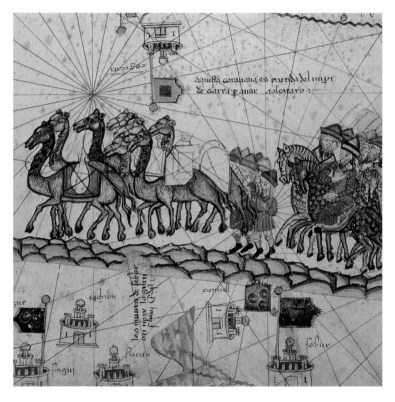

This Catalan map depicts Marco Polo traveling in a caravan with his brother.

which took him four years. He reached further than any explorer to the East, crossing China from west to east, and became the confidant of Kublai Khan, with whom he stayed for twenty years. He saw at first hand the great Chinese civilization, wealth, and sophistication, known only second hand to Westerners through tales and exotic commodities. He saw ginger growing near Sian on his travels in 1280–90. He returned home

Ieuu le souuarä
comeuraens et
suuuere parfaite.
en quoy toutes
choses visibles et
nuisibles passees presentes et ad
uenir maunfestement et aperte
ment apprent. Et deuez sauoir
que du mouuement et uerbera
tion de celly pur air et pure su
uuer naist la parolle dieu. car
parolle nest austre chose que voix
fourmee par uerberation et par

mouuement dair. Et sachies ÿ
dieu est sa parolle, et sa parolle est
dieu. Et est ceste parolle complie
et parfaite par m. souueraumes
dictuures. sans lesquelles dictuure
la parolle dieu cest a dire la dite
ne puet estre acoplie ne parfaite
enterement. Et por ce dist platons.
tons. que ces m. dictuures sont vn
souuerain bien pranapal. le ql
est comeneement de tous aultres
biens et de qui toutes choses pre
deut comenchement et perfection

in 1298, and his subsequent account of his travels was thought to be a work of fiction as it was considered too fabulous to be true.

MEDIEVAL EUROPE

In medieval Europe, ginger was thought to have originated in the Garden of Eden—a beneficial substance created by God at the very beginning of time to be pleasing to humankind. By the tenth century, ginger and cloves, among other Oriental spices, were being sold in the marketplace at Mainz in Germany, brought there by Radanites—Jewish traders who traded warm clothes and white slaves with the East in exchange for spices and precious stones. This was reported by the Moorish physician-merchant, Ibrahim ibn Yaacub, from Mainz.

By the eleventh century, ginger was well known in England. Two centuries later, the returning Crusaders traded with Arab merchants and brought back to England spices including ginger, cinnamon, cloves, and nutmeg. By the fashionable rich they were used more than pepper in cooking, as well as to fight disease and disguise odors.

Crystalizing ginger began in the fourteenth century, when sugar rather than honey started to be used more widely. In that century it was reported that in Europe one pound of ginger could be traded for a sheep.

THE SPICE ROUTE

In the fifteenth and sixteenth centuries, the desire to become rich from trade prompted global discovery. Keen to monopolize the trade in and transport of spices and herbs to the West, the Portuguese financed sailing expeditions to forge a sea route between Portugal and India, China, and the Spice Islands (the Indonesian and Philippine islands). Vasco da Gama was the first European to sail to India in 1497–8, sailing east via the Cape of Good Hope at the foot of Africa. The Portuguese established a

Opposite: A fifteenth-century book illumination showing Adam and Eve in the Garden of Eden.

lucrative trading station in India, which was destroyed two years later by local Moslems.

In 1480, the Italian, Christopher Columbus, decided to travel west to reach China. He failed spectacularly in this mission, but discovered America instead. In the following generation, the Portuguese Ferdinand Magellan thought that he could find a westward route via Cape Horn to the Spice Islands and was commissioned in 1519 by the Spanish, who were trying to outdo Portugal for trade domination. Magellan took with him Antonio Pigafetta, a scholar who noted all the

Ferdinand Magellan was a key player in the race to find a westward route to the Spice Islands.

events of that journey, including the fact that ashore he witnessed ginger being eaten "in a green state ... in the same manner as bread."

In 1561 John Hawkins, an Elizabethan sailor, launched England into the

Right:
John Hawkins: English sailor, adventurer and slave trader.

slave trade by trading 300 slaves at Hispaniola in the West Indies for ginger, pearls, and sugar.

The Spaniards introduced ginger into Jamaica and other parts of the West Indies, and in 1585 the first ginger from Jamaica arrived in Europe.

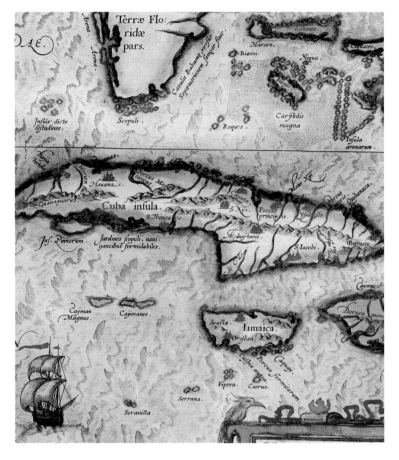

A sixteenth-century map of the West Indies.

The sea route to the Spice Islands became increasingly important as the overland silk routes became impassable, and from about 1650 the silk route fell into disuse.

RENAISSANCE HERBALS

By the time of the European Renaissance in the fifteenth and sixteenth centuries, the amassed knowledge of Greece, Rome,

Portuguese ships
on their way to
the Spice Islands
in 1532.

and Arabia, together with the practical experience of generations
of old wives and apothecaries, had been common currency in
Europe for centuries. Men of the Renaissance started to take a
real interest in discovering how the human body worked, and
what caused disease and how to treat it. Even though

Renaissance men might ultimately discard earlier treatises on the composition of the human body by way of studies of anatomy and dissection, the legacy of the ancients lives on even today. At this time, Elizabethan England, Spain, Portugal, and Holland were in a great race to conquer the world, control spice and silk routes, and expand their geographical and economic boundaries. This set wider the horizons of physicians and scientists who set out to discover and catalog the plant world.

Elizabeth I, a Renaissance queen, was an influential player in the race to conquer the world.

NICHOLAS CULPEPER

Nicholas Culpeper (1616–54) was a seventeenth-century herbalist whose name continues to have resonance at the millennium. His major work, *The English Physitian: enlarged with 369 medicines made of English Herbs*, referred to as the *Herbal*, published in 1653, is still in print to this day, testament to his belief that the individual should be allowed to take part in his

Nicholas Culpeper, Renaissance herbalist and astrologer.

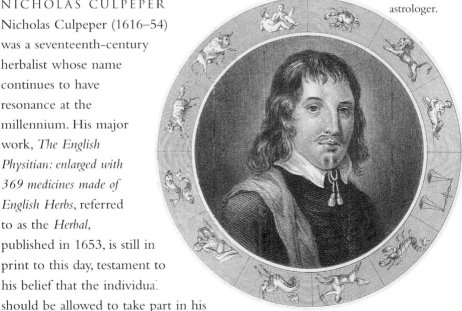

or her own cure. The College of Physicians took against him when he translated their *Pharmacopoeia* into English. This enabled ordinary people to read and understand it—and avoid the need to pay out gross sums to physicians by finding their own herbal medicines in the hedgerows and fields. His own work was a step further in the same direction.

Culpeper gives a surprisingly small description of ginger given the zeal with which the herb was greeted in England at this time.

GINGER

Description. It is very singular in its manner of growth. It produces two kinds of stalks, one bearing the leaves, and the other only the flowers. The first grow two or three feet high, and are themselves composed, in a manner, of the lower parts of leaves; so that they seem to be only bundles of leaves rolled together at the bottom. These are long, narrow, and in some degree resemble the leaves of our common flags [irises]. The other stalks are tender, soft, and about a foot high: they have no leaves on them, but only a kind of films [sic], and at the tops they produce the flowers, in a spike: these are small, in shape like those of our orchis [sic], and of a mixed colour, purple, white, and yellow. The root spreads irregularly under the surface.

Place. It is an East India plant, found also in other places.

Virtues. The root is the only part used: we have it dry at the grocers: but the best way of taking it, is as it comes over preserved from the East Indies. It is a warm and fine stomachic, and dispeller of wind. It assists digestion, and prevents or cures colics. It is also an excellent addition to the rough purges, to prevent their griping in the operation.

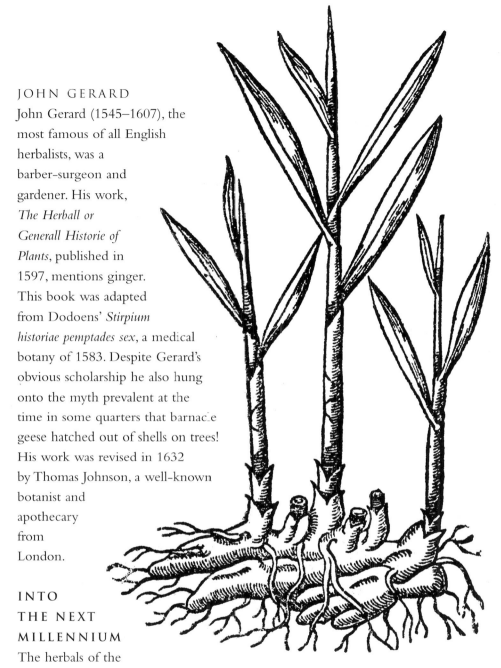

JOHN GERARD

John Gerard (1545–1607), the most famous of all English herbalists, was a barber-surgeon and gardener. His work, *The Herball or Generall Historie of Plants*, published in 1597, mentions ginger. This book was adapted from Dodoens' *Stirpium historiae pemptades sex*, a medical botany of 1583. Despite Gerard's obvious scholarship he also hung onto the myth prevalent at the time in some quarters that barnacle geese hatched out of shells on trees! His work was revised in 1632 by Thomas Johnson, a well-known botanist and apothecary from London.

INTO THE NEXT MILLENNIUM

The herbals of the Renaissance, including that of Culpeper, were in mainstream medical use up until the development of the modern drug industry in the nineteenth century. During this time, chemists analyzed and understood the constituents of herbs

An illustration of ginger from Gerard's *Herball*.

and their essential oils, and were able to introduce new drugs based on chemicals rather than natural substances. While medical chemists confirmed traditional therapeutic uses of many herbs, and the efficacy of traditional remedies, medicine passed into the hands of the professional, and home-made herbal remedies lost their credibility.

PHARMACOGNOSY

Pharmacognosy is the study of natural substances (mainly plants) that are used to make medicines. It is a branch of the science of pharmacology. The word pharmacognosy derives from the Greek *pharmakon* for drug and *gignosco* which means "to acquire knowledge of." The word was probably first used by one Johann Adam Schmidt (1759–1809) in his handwritten volume *Lehrbuch der Materia Medica*, published in Vienna in 1811. Schmidt was also famous as Beethoven's physician, to whom the composer dedicated his trio for piano, clarinet, or violin, and cello (opus 38).

The overwhelming majority of the world's population still relies on remedies of botanical origin for their medicine. By the beginning of the twentieth century, scientists were concerned with describing and identifying drugs and their history, collection, preparation, and storage. There has been a revival in interest in medicinal plants within the scientific community since the 1970s, with companies investing greatly in traditional remedies, largely of botanical origin.

Scientists and researchers have traveled the globe to visit tribal societies in order to examine and chart their traditional folkloric remedies before their cultures decline; this is particularly important in the case of South American tribes, whose culture is rapidly being eroded. Their experience is of huge importance to pharmacologists whose job it is to make new drugs; over centuries such cultures have developed a

knowledge of which herbs are valuable and how to use them.
While scientists have confirmed the pharmacological
effectiveness of many herbal treatments, in some cases their

Acupuncture
students receiving
training in herbal
medicine in
Jakarta, Indonesia.

side-effects have been considered too great by modern Western standards.

In the educational community universities are setting up courses in herbal medicine, notably at Middlesex, which established the first degree course in Britain. The University of Exeter inaugurated its Centre of Complementary Health Studies in 1987. Within the European Community much attention is being paid to drawing up legislation to control the sale, quality and efficacy of herbal medicines that are commercially available.

Opposite:
The Chinese goddess Ma Kou gathering medicinal herbs.

MYTHOLOGY

Those who know the formulas of herbs will say that only medicine will make life unending. They fail in their pursuit of Tao because they are so one-sided. People of superficial knowledge think they have enough when they happen to know of only one way and do not realize that the true seeker will search unceasingly even after he has acquired some good formulas.

Ko Hung, Taoist, c. AD400

China has an exceedingly rich cultural heritage, which includes many myths from varying traditions. Taoism, originally a philosophy, took on the trappings of religion and adopted the Yellow Emperor, Huang Di, as its founder as well as the guru Lao Tzu. Taoism developed its own mythology in line with its own belief system for a healthy way of life. A central tenet of Taoism is that there is only one spiritual path to take through life; if you choose the right one, understand it, and live in harmony with it then wisdom and enlightenment will come to you.

The lifelong goal of some Taoists was to find the elixir of immortality, and myths developed telling stories about ordinary people who had become immortal by following good Taoist practices and who had therefore become capable of performing magical deeds.

THE ELIXIR OF IMMORTALITY

In a Taoist myth, Ti Kuai Li, a learned man and Taoist teacher who was immortal, needed to travel to Wah Shan mountain to visit Lao Tzu, a wise man and teacher. He told his student Li Chang that his spirit would make the journey and that his body would remain with Li Chang. Although the journey was immense, he said that it would take him only seven days to return. Indeed, should he not return within seven days, Li Chang should burn his body. For six days Li Chang waited; on the seventh day his master showed no sign of returning, so Li Chang burned his master's body.

Li Chang was then urgently called away to see his dying mother. Close by he saw a beggar—filthy, bedraggled and deformed—dying at the side of the road. The beggar died with Li Chang at his side. In his haste to reach his mother's bedside, Li Chang had no time to bury the beggar.

While he was away, the spirit of Ti Kuai Li returned from his journey but could not find his body. Eventually he surmised that the burning remains were his body. Unless he could enter the body of someone recently dead he would lose his immortality. He saw the body of the dead beggar and realized that he had no choice but to enter his body.

At once he heard the sound of laughter behind him and saw a shriveled old man carrying a bag of herbs and potions. "I know you," he said to Ti Kuai Li. "I will help you. This potion is a magic elixir which soothes pain and heals wounds. Your appearance will frighten people but you will have the power to heal them."

The old herbalist tipped metal powder from the bottle into his hand, and poured water on to it to form a paste. He shaped the paste into a long metal rod.

"Use this crutch to be your support wherever you go. It will never bend or break," said the herbalist, handing Ti Kuai Li the bottle of potion and the crutch. "You will be immortal from this day forward, but now I must go," he added. "I must return to Lao Tzu as I am his messenger."

At that moment, as the herbalist left, Ti Kuai Li—whose name means god or spirit—realized that he had been in Lao Tzu's presence, and from that day on he traveled the land in the form of a beggar, healing the sick and defending the poor.

CHAPTER 2

REMEDIES

... IT IS OF AN HEATING AND DIGESTING
QUALITIE, AND IS PROFITABLE FOR THE
STOMACKE.

JOHN GERARD, 1597

Herbal medicines at Thalat–Yai market in Savannakhet, Laos.

Ginger has been valued as an ingredient in herbal remedies for 4,000 years: a supreme pedigree. It has traditionally been used as a warming treatment for chills, and also for digestion and flatulence, as well as a way to revive male sex drive. In the eighteenth century its beneficial effect on the digestion was exploited by adding it to many other remedies to soften their effect on the stomach. A number of clinical trials and studies have recently been done on the therapeutic uses of ginger as a tonic for nausea—and particularly for sickness in pregnancy.

Ginger also reduces joint pain in rheumatoid arthritis sufferers; increases bile secretion, thereby improving digestion; increases the strength of the heartbeat; stops blood clotting; stimulates the uterus; and reduces blood sugar concentration, important for diabetes. The *British Herbal Pharmacopoeia* currently lists ginger for use as a carminative (to help relieve flatulence, indigestion, and colic), diaphoretic (to increase perspiration), and to prevent sickness. **In excess, ginger may interfere with cardiac, anti-diabetic and anti-coagulant therapy and may cause abortion. It is not to be taken by people with gallstones or gallbladder problems.**

Ginger is non-toxic and non-irritant in amounts normally used in food, but it may cause sensitization so it is important to do a patch test before using any topical applications: apply one or two drops of the preparation to a small area of moderately sensitive skin, such as the inside of the arm. Wait for half an hour to see if any allergic reaction occurs before using it in any other way.

PARTS USED
- rhizome
- essential oil

EFFECTS
- Anti-emetic: helps prevent nausea and vomiting.
- Anti-spasmodic: reduces involuntary spasms in muscles.
- Carminative: relieves indigestion and flatulence.
- Antiseptic: controls or prevents bacterial infection.
- Circulatory stimulant: improves blood flow.
- Diaphoretic: increases perspiration.
- Expectorant: makes coughing productive.
- Peripheral vasodilator: dilates blood vessels in the extremities, thereby improving circulation.

Three different
forms of ginger:
from top to
bottom, the root,
dried ginger, and
ginger capsules.

CONSTITUENTS

Starch (up to 50 per cent), lipids (6–8 per cent), oleo-resin (up to
33 per cent), volatile oils (1–3 per cent), amino acids, protein
(c. 9 per cent), resins, vitamins (especially vitamin A and niacin),
minerals.

FORMS

Ginger may be taken in the following forms:

- fresh and dried rhizome
- essential oil
- capsules filled with powdered root
- powdered root

- ginger oleoresin BPC
- ginger syrup
- tincture (strong and weak BP formulations)
- ginger juice

ESSENTIAL OIL

The volatile oils of ginger are chemical compounds that are found in the unpeeled ginger rhizome. Upon extraction from other compounds present in the rhizome, it is called essential oil. Essential oils are a very potent and intense way of appreciating the aromatic qualities of a plant, and can reach the human bloodstream in as little as 20 minutes after application to the skin. Essential oils are used in the treatment of muscle pains, digestive disorders, and inflammations. The essential oil of ginger combines well with sandalwood, frankincense, rose, orange, juniper, and eucalyptus.

Essential oils should not be taken internally or used in any form if you are pregnant; great care should be taken with them in the case of breastfeeding or with young children. Do a patch test as essential oils may cause an allergic reaction. Do not use essential oils neat or in diluted form on skin that is to be exposed to direct sunlight, as this can cause pigmentation, inflammation, or other skin damage.

AROMATHERAPY

The term "aromatherapy" was first used in 1928 by René-Maurice Gattefosse, a French chemist working in his family perfume business. He revived the use of essential oils for health and well-being as well as beauty. The story goes that he was working in the laboratory when he burned his hand; he plunged it into a vessel containing lavender oil and discovered that it healed faster and scarred less than he had expected. Dr Jean Valnet took Gattefosse's ideas one stage further, discovering while treating soldiers' wounds during the Second World War that essential oils have antiseptic and regenerative properties. He also used oils to treat specific medical and psychiatric disorders.

Marguerite Maury (1895–1968) took the emerging practice of aromatherapy into the wider arena and, in her book *The Secret of Life and Youth* published in 1964, explained how essential oils could be applied through massage to promote health and beauty. This technique had, of course, been known to ancient Egyptians, Greeks, and Romans, but had lain in the shadows for centuries.

A porter carries harvested ginger rhizomes in West Bengal.

AYURVEDIC AND CHINESE MEDICINE

In Ayurvedic medicine, ginger is used to treat bronchitis, phthisis (pulmonary tuberculosis), rheumatism, and postnatal complaints, and as an anti-emetic (to help prevent nausea and vomiting). The three different body types—*doshas*—all call upon ginger in fresh or dried form to create remedies to treat the conditions to which they may fall prey. Indeed, ginger is included in about half of all prescriptions.

Vata types are defined as tall, thin people who are artistic and sensitive. Their dominant elements are ether and air. It is

Different forms of ginger. From left to right: ground ginger; Thai ginger, *galangal*; root ginger and candied ginger.

recommended that they take ginger tea and other remedies made from fresh ginger. *Pitta* types also benefit from the use of fresh ginger. These are usually people of average build, with the elements of fire and water dominant. They are characterized as impatient and intelligent people subject to strong emotions.

Kapha types are recommended to use dry ginger, perhaps in the form of a warm, spicy yogurt drink flavored with dry ginger, cinnamon, and cloves. These are usually well-built people who are stubborn, motherly, and reliable. Their dominant elements are water and earth.

In Chinese medicine, ginger is valued as a warming remedy.
The fresh root is called *shen jiang*, and is used to encourage
sweating and to rid the body of colds, chills, and coughs. Roasted
in hot ashes, it is used to treat diarrhoea or to stop bleeding. The
dried root is called *gan jiang*, and is used to warm the stomach and
lungs, as well as for abdominal pain and diarrhoea. It restores yang.
The peeled root skin, *jiang pi*, is used for oedema and bloating.

BASIC RECIPES

Ginger may be taken internally, in the form of tisanes, for
example, or externally, as a massage oil. Here we give basic
recipes which anyone can
make. You will need a small
amount of equipment:

* small kitchen scales
* dark glass bottles
* glass jars with airtight lids
* small glass pots with
  airtight lids
* a fine-mesh sieve.

Always wash your hands
thoroughly before starting
work, and use clean and dry
tools uncontaminated with
foods or other herbs.

It is imperative to label
and date any preparation that
you make at home. Include
the following information:
the name of the herb; whether
it is fresh, dried or powdered;
the type of preparation made;
and the date.

Chinese herbs
stored in
airtight jars.

Store all ingredients and preparations out of the reach of children.

If symptoms persist or worsen, consult a professional immediately. Take particular care not to overdose your child: see the recommended doses for children (see below). Take care not to give your child several different treatments at the same time. If you are breastfeeding, remember that whatever you eat or drink finds its way through your milk into your baby, so take care not to take ginger in excess as it may adversely affect both you and your child.

RECOMMENDED DOSES FOR CHILDREN

6 months–1 year	5% of adult dosage
1–3	10%
3–5	20%
5–7	30%
7–9	40%
9–11	50%
11–13	60%
13–15	80%
15 up	100%

Root and ground ginger.

INTERNAL APPLICATIONS

Here are recipes for versatile treatments which may be taken on their own or used as the base for another preparation. For example, a tisane may be drunk or poured into a bath. It is important not to make the recipes any stronger than is described here, not to take too much of the preparation, and not to mix preparations.

In general, when water is included in a recipe, use spring water.

You may use fresh ginger or half the amount of dried ginger in any of these recipes.

TISANE, TEA, OR INFUSION

A tisane is a traditional medicinal preparation: indeed the word is derived from the ancient Greek word for a medicinal brew. This is a simple and popular way of enjoying the therapeutic qualities of ginger.

Put 3 ounces of fresh sliced ginger into a teapot. Pour on 2 cups of freshly boiled water and put the lid on the

teapot to prevent the aromatic constituents from escaping. Allow the ginger to steep for 15 minutes. Then strain the liquid through a sieve straight into a cup for immediate consumption, or into a jug, if you wish to drink it later. Keep the remainder in the fridge to be reheated or drunk cold as you choose. These quantities make three doses, a single day's supply. In Ayurvedic medicine, ginger tea is drunk either hot or at room temperature, not chilled.

Ginger tea is a pleasant and effective remedy for a number of complaints.

For a single cup, use 3 teaspoons of grated ginger to 1 cup of boiling water.

Try combining ginger and apple, or ginger and lemon for a different taste. You may also add a pinch of powdered ginger to other teas.

49

TINCTURE

Strong ginger tincture is a pharmaceutical preparation made by extracting powdered ginger with 90 per cent ethanol (pure alcohol). Vodka is considered unsuitable because it usually consists of about 37½ per cent alcohol and is not strong enough to extract all the flavors. You can buy ready-prepared ginger tinctures from pharmacists or from mail-order companies.

Tinctures last for up to two years since the alcohol acts as a preservative. In this way, ginger can be used even when you do not have fresh ginger to hand.

Peel fresh ginger with a sharp paring knife.

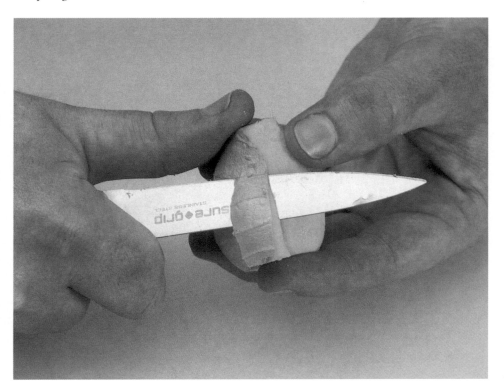

DECOCTION

This is a technique for extracting flavors from the woodier parts of a plant, including roots such as ginger. A decoction needs to be used on the same day as you prepare it.

Put 1 ounce of sliced ginger and 1 cup plus 2 tablespoons of cold water into a saucepan (not aluminum). Bring it to the boil and simmer it for 15–20 minutes, until the volume has reduced by one-third. Strain it through a sieve. Add honey or cinnamon to taste.

SYRUP

This is a useful recipe for treating colds and 'flu.

Mix 2 cups of boiling ginger decoction with 1½ cups of honey. Heat the mixture gently until all the honey has dissolved, then boil it until it thickens.

EXTERNAL APPLICATIONS

Here are some recipes for preparations that may be applied externally. They include treatments that are rubbed in, inhaled, used for massage, and placed directly on wounds.

INFUSED OIL

This recipe is used as a base for making ointments or massage oils.

- For the warm infused method place 10½ ounces of fresh ginger in a bowl over a saucepan containing water, and cover it with 2 cups of olive or sunflower oil. Heat the mixture for about three hours (taking care that the pan does not boil dry). Strain and store the resulting greenish liquid in dark, airtight bottles, away from direct sunlight. Label and date them.
- For cold infused oil steep 1 part of fresh ginger in 5 parts of oil at room temperature for 12 hours. Strain the mixture.

Essential oils made from herbs and flowers are valuable healing resources.

MASSAGE OIL

This is a delightfully warm and stimulating recipe to ease stiffness, aches, and pains, and for use in aromatherapy.

Place 20 drops of ginger essential oil (or a combination of ginger and juniper or eucalyptus) in a dark bottle. Add ¼ cup of jojoba oil. Put the lid on and then roll the bottle gently between the hands to mix the ingredients. Never shake the bottle. Label and date the bottle and store it in a cool, dark place. Alternatively, try mixing ginger with rosewood, sandalwood, or juniper.

Jojoba oil makes the skin feel as smooth as satin.

Alternatively, you could use:

- almond oil: very popular in massage oils
- olive oil: calming and pungent
- hazelnut oil: nourishing and stimulating.

WARMING EXOTIC BATH

For a warming and stimulating bath, grate a ¾ inch cube of fresh ginger, place it in a cheesecloth square, tie the corners together and place it underneath the hot tap in the stream of water. Alternatively mix 5 drops of ginger essential oil in 1 tablespoon of almond oil and add that to the bath water.

Treat yourself to a warming bath with an exotic fragrance.

HOT GINGER COMPRESS

For a warming treatment for rheumatism and muscular pain, fill a bowl with just-boiled water and add 4 drops of ginger essential oil. Soak a clean wash cloth in the liquid, wring it out and place it on the affected part until the liquid has cooled to blood heat. Repeat as you feel necessary, or until the water in the bowl has cooled.

Muscular aches and pains are soothed by a massage with ginger essential oil.

PREGNANCY AND BREASTFEEDING

Pregnant women need to take particular care when using herbal remedies in any way as they may affect the unborn child adversely. Be sure to seek advice from your health professional before taking herbal remedies.

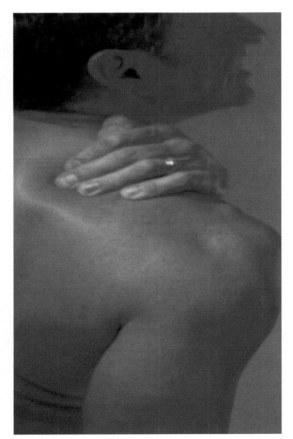

Similarly, breastfeeding women need to be aware that a herb may affect the milk supply and will certainly pass into the child via the milk. The La Leche League, the international charity that offers help and information to women who want to breastfeed, stresses that all herbs should be considered as medication and that in case of any breastfeeding difficulties a mother should seek help straightaway and discuss any herbal remedies she has been taking.

AILMENTS

Ginger has been used over thousands of years to treat a wide range of illnesses including arthritis, fatigue, aches and pains, rheumatism, coughs and 'flu, diarrhoea, flatulence, indigestion, nausea, and nervous exhaustion. Scientists think that ginger may protect the stomach from the damaging effect of alcohol, and may help prevent ulcers, but further research is necessary.

Do not take ginger internally if you have a high fever, an inflammatory skin complaint, ulcers of the digestive tract, or gallstones. For major or persistent problems be sure to consult a qualified herbalist, homeopath, or your doctor.

Aches and pains

If you suffer from muscular aches and pains, have a massage with ginger essential oil, a warm compress or a ginger bath.

The warmth of ginger brings relief to arthritic joints.

Arthritis

Ginger has anti-inflammatory properties, and in this way can bring relief to arthritis sufferers. Have a ginger massage or place a warm compress on the affected part. It also helps to take ginger internally.

Catarrh

To relieve catarrh, take a ginger decoction.

Circulation problems

If you are suffering from poor circulation, a ginger bath or massage warms and stimulates the affected parts.

Colds and chills

To warm the body and provide relief from colds and chills, take
a decoction of ginger. For the most traditional remedy add
1 teaspoon of freshly grated ginger to a cup of hot water; let it
steep for 10 minutes, then add the juice of half a lemon and
1 teaspoon of honey, with perhaps a splash or two of whiskey.

Colic

An older baby or child may be given a weak ginger tea to drink
(see Recommended doses for children, page 48) if she has colic
or a sore tummy, or is teething. Alternatively, give the child a
massage with very dilute ginger essential oil (see page 52).

Cramp in the stomach

To ease the pain of gastric cramp and spasms, apply a hot ginger
compress or have a ginger stomach massage.

A warming ginger
massage is
an effective
treatment for
various conditions,
such as circulation
problems
and cramps.

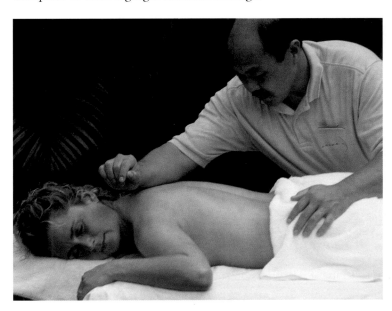

Diarrhoea

To calm the stomach, drink a cup of warm ginger tea or apply a warm ginger compress.

Fatigue

To relieve fatigue, have a massage including ginger essential oil. A warming and fragrant ginger bath is also effective in helping you to relax and restore your energy.

Feverish chill

Take a cup of ginger decoction to warm the body if you are suffering from a feverish chill. Alternatively, apply a warm ginger compress to your forehead or chest.

Flatulence

Take up to 10 drops of ginger tincture to ease flatulence.

Indigestion

Ginger increases the production of digestive fluids and saliva, and in this way can help prevent or soothe indigestion. It is not, however, to be taken by those with gallstones or gallbladder problems.

Take up to 10 drops of tincture. Alternatively, steep 1 teaspoon of grated fresh ginger in 1 cup of just boiled water for 10 minutes. Drink while the water is still warm.

Migraine headache

To alleviate a migraine headache, take a ginger decoction or rub a little ginger massage oil into the temples.

Morning sickness

Morning sickness is absolutely miserable, and the gravity and longevity of it usually comes as a shock to pregnant women. It is a consolation to know that clinical trials have shown dried ginger to

be successful in treating very severe pregnancy sickness *(hyperemesis gravidarum)*. It is quite simply considered to be the best remedy around. However, the German Federal Health Agency has issued a note of caution: pregnant women should avoid excessive doses of ginger because it may inhibit testosterone binding in the growing foetus. Although no studies have proved this, Commission E currently contraindicates ginger for morning sickness, but this is being disputed. In any event, long-term use of ginger is not recommended as it is also reputedly abortifacient and a uterine stimulant in excess (see page 42). In general, if symptoms persist, do consult your health professional to ensure that both you and the baby are monitored.

Opposite: Ginger is the best remedy available for very severe and persistent pregnancy sickness.

To alleviate the symptoms of morning sickness, try drinking a cup of ginger tea up to three times a day, munching a piece of candied ginger or taking 10 drops of tincture in a cup of warm water. Take prescribed doses of medication containing ginger, and seek professional advice rather than opting for self-medication.

Muscular pain

To relieve muscular pain, massage a blend of ginger with other essential oils (see page 44) into the affected area. Alternatively, apply a hot ginger compress.

A cup of ginger tea can ease nausea and vomiting.

Nausea and vomiting

Ginger is the best remedy for nausea of all kinds, including sickness in pregnancy (see page 59) and travel sickness in children. Its action in promoting gastrointestinal circulation makes it the most useful herbal remedy in this

regard. Hospitals in Denmark and the UK conducting clinical studies into the effectiveness of ginger have confirmed its usefulness in both motion sickness and in preventing post-operative nausea.

Take a cup of ginger tea (see page 49) or 10 drops of tincture. Ginger capsules may also be taken to ease travel sickness.

Nervous exhaustion

A warming ginger bath helps to bring relief to someone suffering from nervous exhaustion or tension.

Menstrual pain

Drinking ginger tea or applying a hot ginger compress or massage
will soothe some of the cramps associated with menstrual pain.

Rheumatism

For effective and warming relief from rheumatism and aching
bones, rub ginger massage oil into the affected part. Alternatively,
apply a hot ginger compress (see page 54).

Sinusitis

Ginger and peppermint tincture, combined in equal parts, is also
a good treatment.

Sprains and strains

Apply a warm ginger compress or have a massage with ginger
essential oil to bring relief from sprains and strains.

Throat problems

If you have a sore throat, a cup of warm ginger tea with added
honey. If symptoms persist, do consult your health professional.

Varicose veins

If you suffer from varicose veins, massage gently around the area
with infused oil of ginger, avoiding the veins themselves.

Opposite:
Sinusitis is eased
after a ginger
steam inhalation.

CHAPTER 3

COSMETICS AND SCENTED DECORATIONS

YOU SPREAD A TABLE FOR ME IN FULL VIEW OF MY ENEMIES. YOU ANOINT MY HEAD WITH OIL; MY CUP IS BRIM-FULL. ONLY GOODNESS AND MERCY WILL FOLLOW ME ALL THE DAYS OF MY LIFE, AND I SHALL LIVE IN THE LORD'S HOUSE FOR MANY, MANY YEARS.

PSALM 23

The warming and aromatic qualities of ginger may be harnessed just as effectively by making cosmetics and scented decorations as by taking herbal remedies. Indeed, in centuries past, no distinction was drawn between medical and cosmetic uses: they were considered to be in the same category.

This chapter contains inspiration to make your own cosmetics and scented decorations. You will probably have a lot of fun, and will enjoy the results of your work.

Opposite:
A Roman flask (c. AD250) and a glass Roman aryballos (c. AD100) used for storing and using perfumed oils.

MAKING YOUR OWN COSMETICS

Here is a collection of simple recipes for you to make your own cosmetics Try the ones that appeal, and then don't be afraid to experiment. Ginger combines well with juniper, eucalyptus, sandalwood, and rose for a warming and exotic aroma.

Be aware that sensitive skins may have an adverse allergic reaction, so always do a patch test (see page 42) before using your home-made cosmetic.

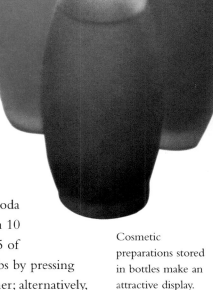

GINGER BATH FIZZ

For a stimulating and warming bath fizz try the following recipe. Mix together 1 cup of baking soda with 1 tablespoon of citric acid. Then sprinkle in 10 drops of ginger essential oil (or 5 of ginger and 5 of juniper). Mix together. You may make bath bombs by pressing the mixture into an egg cup until it holds together; alternatively, sprinkle a handful directly into the bath.

Cosmetic preparations stored in bottles make an attractive display.

HAIR RINSE

To give brown hair a red tone, rinse it with ginger tea after shampooing.

PERFUME

To make an exotic perfume, put 6 drops of jasmine essential oil and 6 of sandalwood with 2 drops of ginger and 2 of mint essential oil into a ¼ cup bottle. Add 7 teaspoons of vodka, seal it, and leave it for two days. Then add 3 teaspoons of spring water. Reseal it and leave it for six weeks before using it.

MAKING YOUR OWN SCENTED ITEMS

You can make your own scented decorations quite simply. They are a pleasure to make, either for yourself or as gifts, and you can use your own creativity in choosing fabrics, ribbons, lace, or any other trimmings you like. You need not do a great deal of sewing. If you do get out your sewing machine, ensure that you leave one edge of the fabric easy to undo so that you can open it up to revitalize the pot-pourri mixture with a drop or two of essential oil every couple of months.

EXOTIC POT-POURRI

For an exotic pot-pourri blend, mix slices of dried ginger with cinnamon sticks, juniper berries and sandalwood shavings. For every 4 cups volume of plant material, add 1 tablespoon of orris root to fix the perfume, and 5 drops of ginger essential oil. Store the pot-pourri in a sealed container in a warm, dark place for six weeks, shaking it occasionally. You may top up the essential oils after the pot-pourri has been displayed for a few months, if you need to reinvigorate it.

SCENTED CUSHION

Make a cushion cover out of the fabric of your choice, leaving one side unstitched. Half fill the cushion with kapok filling. Then add a bag of exotic pot-pourri (see page 64), add more kapok filling, and sew shut the last side.

Alternatively, a simpler approach is to make a small cheesecloth square, fill it with exotic pot-pourri and tuck it inside your cushion covers. Every time you lean against the cushions you will release a warming scent.

SCENTED SACHETS

To make clothes sachets with a warm, enticing scent, to hang in a wardrobe or put in a drawer where they will aerate and perfume your clothes, place pot-pourri mix in a square of fabric. Gather together the corners and tie them with ribbon or lace, leaving a loop by which to hang it if you choose to place the sachet over a clothes hanger in the wardrobe.

WARMING GINGER ROOM SPRAY

For a fragrant room spray pour 2 cups of boiling water onto 12 tablespoons of grated fresh ginger. Cool and strain the mixture. Then mix it with $^2/_3$ cup of vodka. Add 10 drops of ginger essential oil, or a combination of ginger and rose. Store it in a dark glass bottle, clearly labeled and dated.

BATH SCENTER

Grate a walnut-sized piece of fresh ginger into a square of cheesecloth. Tie the cheesecloth with a ribbon and loop it over the hot tap so that the warm water runs through the bag.

Opposite:
An exotic pot-pourri of ginger and spices is fun to make and pleasurable to scent.

SCENTED CANDLE

A scented candle may be made in several ways. Most simply, light a wide candle and let the top of the wax melt. Put out the flame and mix a few drops of ginger essential oil into the melted wax. The fragrance should last for an hour.

Alternatively, you may buy a candle-making kit and add ginger essential oil to the mixture just before pouring it into the candle mold.

Opposite:
Ginger-scented candles release a delightful aroma and create a relaxing ambience.

CHAPTER 4
GINGER
FLAVORINGS

RUN, RUN, AS FAST AS YOU CAN. YOU CAN'T

CATCH ME, I'M THE GINGERBREAD MAN!

ENGLISH FOLK TALE

Traditional
gingerbread
men are fun to
make and eat.

Ginger has been prized as a flavoring for as long as it has been used in medicinal remedies. In fact, candied ginger may be used equally as a tasty foodstuff and a remedy for nausea.

Ginger has also been a valued ingredient in drinks since medieval times, when it was first used to flavor ales. By 1800 it became a popular soft drink—ginger beer—in its own right, and was taken up on a large scale by the temperance movement. It was particularly popular in Britain in the early 1900s with

Preserved ginger (top), dried and candied (bottom) are prized flavorings in food and drink.

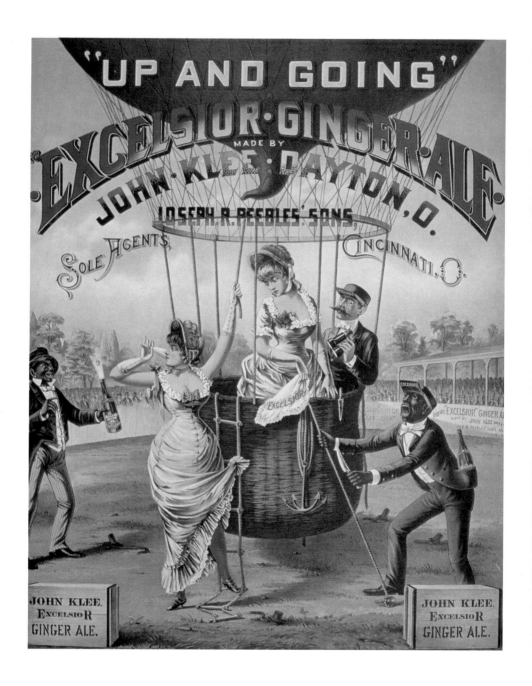

miners and their families. However, in the 1960s and 1970s the factories making it closed down. Now, however, there is a revival in the fortunes of this refreshing and sweet soft drink, and in the USA ginger ale is competing hard with iced tea as a popular non-alcoholic beverage.

Opposite:
A nineteenth-century advertisement for Excelsior Ginger Ale.

CANDIED GINGER

Candied ginger is delicious, whether eaten as a remedy for nausea, as a sweet treat or as part of a recipe. It is also easy and fun to make.

Take 9 ounces of young, fresh ginger, peel it and slice it thinly. Place it in a saucepan, add water to cover it and simmer it gently for about half an hour until it is tender.

Drain the ginger, then weigh it again and put it back in the saucepan with its own weight of sugar and 1½ tablespoons of water. Bring it to the boil, stirring it regularly, until most of the liquid has evaporated and the ginger is transparent. At this point, turn the heat down and, stirring constantly, cook it further until it is almost dry.

Remove the ginger from the heat altogether and toss it in more sugar to coat it. Let it cool and store it in an airtight jar. Label and date the jar. Candied ginger stores for up to three months.

MARGOT'S GINGER BEER

This is a very old recipe for a fizzy, peppery soft drink. It is fun—and educational—for both children and adults to make during the long summer vacation as it can become an ongoing project. The quantities listed here make about 15 quarts of ginger beer.

First you need to make the ginger beer "plant". Mix together 1 cup of sugar, 1 tablespoon of ground ginger, the juice of

2 lemons, and 1 quart of water. Most of the sugar should
dissolve. Place the mixture in a large, open-necked jar; put the lid
on it and allow it to stand for three days. Then pour off nearly all
the liquid and, in order to establish fermentation, feed it daily for
at least seven days with 1 large teaspoon of sugar and 1 level
teaspoon of ground ginger.

To make the ginger beer itself, use a container large enough
to hold 15 quarts. Put in 2 pounds 3 ounces of sugar, and
4½ cups of boiling water. Stir the mixture until all the sugar has
dissolved. Then add 1 cup of strained lemon juice, 2¼ cups of
the ginger beer plant mixture, and 1 dessertspoon of ground
ginger. Stir this well. Add 11½ quarts of cold water, stir well and
cover.

After about two hours, stir the mixture again, recover it, and
leave it to stand for 24 hours without moving it. After this time,
strain all the clear liquid through cheesecloth in a sieve, retaining
the sediment for later. Pour the liquid into recycled plastic drink
bottles. NB: It is essential to use plastic bottles as glass ones have
been known to explode in storage. In its heyday ginger beer
would have been served out of stone jars, strong enough to
withstand any build-up of pressure.

The ginger beer may be drunk after three days. Open the
bottles extremely slowly to allow the gas to escape safely.

To start a new ginger beer plant, put all the sediment back
into the open-necked jar, cover it, and feed it daily as you did in
the beginning.

GREAT GRANDFATHER'S GINGER WINE

This is another old recipe, which my pharmacist grandfather
used to make. It was sold in the family pharmacy in a mining
community in the north-east of England, as well as consumed by
his own family.

Opposite:
An Owambo
woman from
Namibia carrying
a jar of ginger
beer on her head.

Le Petit Journal

SUPPLÉMENT ILLUSTRÉ

Le Petit Journal
CHAQUE JOUR 5 CENTIMES
Le Supplément illustré
CHAQUE SEMAINE 5 CENTIMES

Huit pages : CINQ centimes

ABONNEMENTS

	SIX MOIS	UN AN
SEINE ET SEINE-ET-OISE	2 fr.	3 fr. 50
DÉPARTEMENTS	2 fr.	4 fr.
ÉTRANGER	2 50	5 fr.

Huitième année

DIMANCHE 27 JUIN 1897

Numéro 3

(Phot. W. et D. Downey, Lond.)

JUBILÉ DE LA REINE D'ANGLETERRE

Sa Majesté Victoria, Reine d'Angleterre, Impératrice des Indes

Dissolve ¼ ounce of tartaric acid (available from your pharmacist) in a little water; add 1 quart of syrup and 1½ cups of sherry. Stir well.

Then add 2½ teaspoons of strong ginger tincture (available from your pharmacist or mail-order supplier), 1 scant teaspoon of tincture of capsicum (similarly available), and 1 tablespoon of lemon juice. Stir well.

Add caramel (from your pharmacist) to taste and color the liquid as you desire. Then mix well with 2 quarts of water.

Bottle the mixture, label, and date it.

Opposite: A French magazine in celebration of Queen Victoria's Diamond Jubilee in 1897.

JUBILEE POP

I have turned up a delightful recipe for Jubilee Pop, developed to celebrate Queen Victoria's Diamond Jubilee in 1897. It has a warm, fruity taste and a pretty red-orange color. Jubilee Pop was originally made with soluble essences of ginger, lemon, and orange, which first came on the market in the 1870s and are still available in some pharmacies today. As an alternative use fruit cordials to make the recipe.

Mix together ¼ cup of ginger cordial, 2 tablespoons of lemon cordial, and 1 tablespoon of orange cordial together with 1 tablespoon of red food coloring and 4.5 litres quarts of spring water.

Dissolve 2 ounces of tartaric acid in 1¼ cups of rosewater, and add this solution to the mixture. Add a little orange coloring, and mix well together.

FURTHER READING

Arber, A., *Herbals: Their Origin and Evolution; A Chapter in the History of Botany, 1470–1670*, Cambridge University Press, New York, 1987

Bown, D., *The Encyclopedia of Herbs and Their Uses*, DK, New York, 1995

Bremness, L., *Crabtree & Evelyn Fragrant Herbal: Enhancing Your Life with Aromatic Herbs and Essential Oils*, Bullfinch, Boston, 1998

Campbell, Joseph, *The Mask of God: Oriental Mythology*, Arkana New York, 1991

Culpeper, N., *Culpeper's Complete Herbal & English Physician*, Meyerbooks, Glenwood, Illinois 1987

Evans, W. C., *Trease and Evans' Pharmacognosy*, W. B. Saunders, London, 1996

Gao, Duo, *The Encyclopedia of Chinese Medicine*, Sevenoaks, 1997

Hillier, M., *The Little Scented Library: Sachets and Cushions*, DK, New York, 1992

Lawless, J., *The Illustrated Encyclopedia of Essential Oils: The Complete Guide to The Use of Oils in Aromatherapy and Herbalism*, Element, Boston, 1995

Lewis, Walter H. and Elvin-Lewis, Memory P. F., *Medical Botany: Plants Affecting Man's Health*, John Wiley and Sons, New York, 1982.

MacEwan, Peter, *Pharmaceutical Formulas: A Book of Useful Recipes for the Drug Trade*, The Chemist and Druggist, London, 1899

Milton, Giles, *Nathaniel's Nutmeg*, Farrar, Straus and Giroux, New York, 1999

Morningstar, Sally, *Ayurveda: Traditional Indian Healing for Harmony and Health*, Anness Publishing, New York, 1999.

Nice, J., *Herbal Remedies for Healing: A Complete A–Z of Ailments and Treatments*, Piatkus, London, 1991

Ody, P., *Simple Healing with Herbs: Herbal Treatments for More Than 100 Common Ailments*, Storey Publishing, Williamstown, Massachusetts, 1999

Ody, P., *The Complete Medicinal Herbal*, DK, New York, 1993

Palmer, M., and Zhao Xiaomin, *Essential Chinese Mythology*, Thorsons, London, 1997

Shaw, N., *Herbalism: An Illustrated Guide*, Element, Boston, 1999

Trager, James, *The Food Chronology*, Henry Holt, New York, 1997

Tyler, Varro E. et al, *Pharmacognosy*, Lea & Febiger, New York

ACKNOWLEDGEMENTS

Thanks go to Deni Bown, for her comments and expertise, to Frances
Vargo and Margot Richardson for their invaluable contributions to the
book, and to my father, Brian Ferry, as well as Rachel al-Azzawi and Nina
Payne for their help and encouragement. Particular thanks are due to
Richard, who provided me with great support and opportunities to write
in such as way that Matilda didn't realize Mummy was busy.
Margot's Ginger Beer recipe copyright © Margot Richardson. Used with
permission.

PICTURE ACKNOWLEDGEMENTS

The publishers would like to thank the following sources for their kind
permission to reproduce the pictures in this book:

The AncientArt & Architecture Collection Ltd 17, 18; **AKG London** 6,
19, 20tl, 22, 26, 28tl, 30, 31tl, 76; **The Bridgeman Art Library,**
London/Stapleton Collection Anciente Rome, from 'The Art of Perfume', pub.
1912 (pochoir print) by Georges Barbier (1882-1932) 20br , The Banquet of
Mark Anthony and Cleopatra by Francesco Trevisani (1556-1746) Galleria degli
Uffizi, Florence, Italy, 21br , Flask, Roman, c.250AD, areballos with chain,
Roman, c.100 AD (glass) Freud Museum, London 62; **Carlton Books Ltd** 40,
43, 48; **Cephas Picture Library**/TOP/Christian Adam 46; **Corbis**/Zen
Icknow 16b, Archivo Iconografico s.a., 29, Bettmann 72, Macduff Everton 56,
Peter Johnson 74; **Mary Evans Picture Library** 15, 21t, 23, 31br, 33, 36; **et
archive** 14, 24, 16tl, 25, 28br; **Food Features** 50, 71; **Werner Forman Archive**
24br; **The Image Bank** 54, 55, 60, 63, 65; **Images Colour Library** 47; **Panos
Pictures** Jean-Leo Dugast 41, Jeremy Hartley 35, Sean Sprague 10, 45; **Retna
Pictures Ltd** 66, JennyAcheson 68; **Harry Smith Horticultural Photographic
Collection** 8; **Science Photo Library** 52; **Dawson Strange Photography** 49;
Tony Stone Images/ Laurence Monneret 58, 9, 12, 53, 59, 70

Every effort has been made to acknowledge correctly and contact the source
and/copyright holder of each picture, and Carlton Books Limited apologises for
any unintentional errors or omissions which will be corrected in future editions
of this book.